LET'S INVESTIGATE
Shape Patterns

LET'S INVESTIGATE
Shape
Patterns

By Marion Smoothey

Illustrated by Ted Evans

MARSHALL CAVENDISH
NEW YORK · LONDON · TORONTO · SYDNEY

Library Edition Published 1993

© Marshall Cavendish Corporation 1993

Published by Marshall Cavendish Corporation
2415 Jerusalem Avenue
PO Box 587
North Bellmore
New York 11710

Series created by Graham Beehag Book Design

Library of Congress Cataloging-in-Publication Data

Smoothey, Marion, 1943-
    Shape patterns / by Marion Smoothey; illustrated by Ted Evans.
      p. cm.. -- (Let's Investigate)
    Includes index.
    Summary: Explores the world of shapes and how they can be drawn, measured, and used in various activities.
    ISBN 1-85435-465-5 ISBN 1-85435-463-9 (set)
    1. Geometry -- Juvenile literature. 2. Symmetry -- Juvenile literature
    [1. Shape. 2. Geometry.]
    I. Evans, Ted ill. II. Title. III. Series:
    Smoothey, Marion, 1943- Let's Investigate.
    QA445.5.565 1993   92-36223
    516' . 15---dc20   CIP
                                      AC

Printed in Singapore by Times Offset PTE Ltd
Bound in the United States

Contents

Many of the patterns in this book are based on a grid, or framework, of dots in a square or triangular pattern. To save time and trouble, you can copy the grids on page 59, or buy graph paper.

You will need tracing paper and a small mirror with a straight edge.

A pencil, a ruler and some colored pencils are all you need to make the patterns.

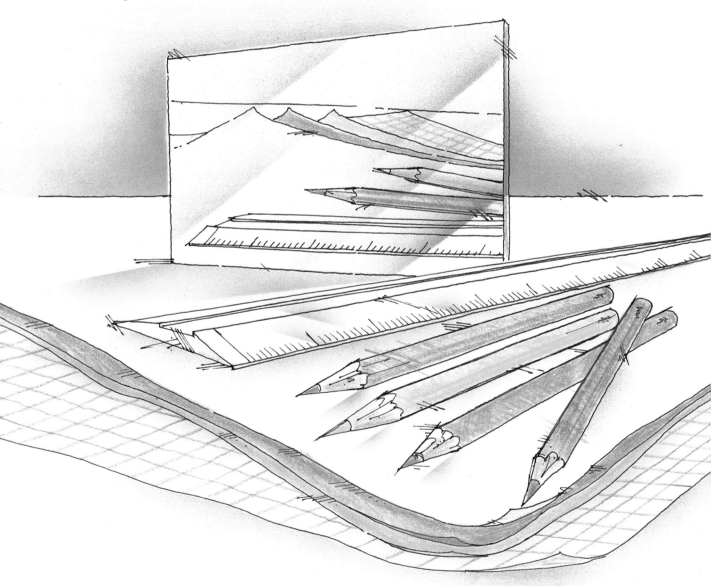

Spirobots

Spirobots draw patterns on graph paper as they move. They can be programmed to move a set number of squares and to turn 90° right or left. Each spirorobot displays its program. When a spirobot returns to its starting position, it stops.

This is the pattern that this spirorobot draws.

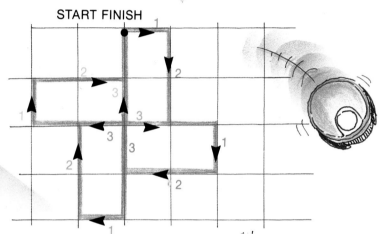

START FINISH

1. Using graph paper, try drawing this spirobot's pattern.

● What do you notice?

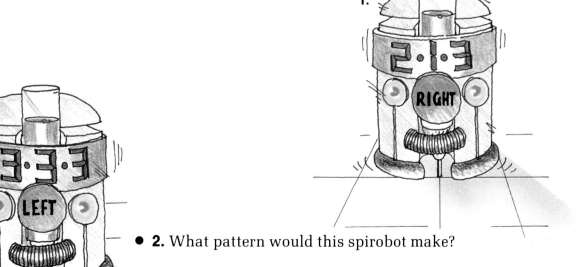

● **2.** What pattern would this spirobot make?

1. You should have found that 1, 2, 3 right and 2, 1, 3 right produce the same patterns but with different starting points.

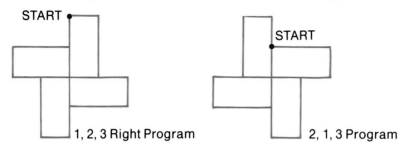

START •

1, 2, 3 Right Program

START •

2, 1, 3 Program

2. The spirobot with the 3, 3, 3 left moves only four distances before it stops. It makes a square.

3, 3, 3 Left Program

This spirobot has a longer program and a more complicated pattern.

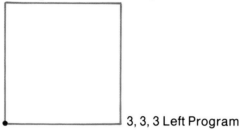

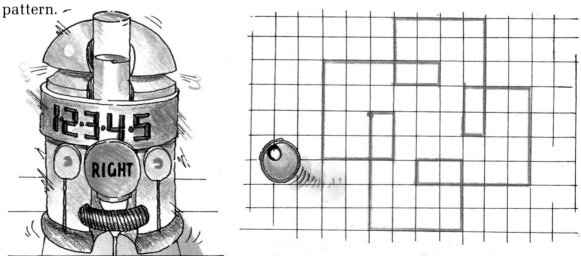

● **3.** How many times does it repeat the program before it returns to the starting point?

● **4. a)** Try to draw a 2, 1, 4 left pattern on graph paper.

● **b)** How many times must you repeat the sequence of turns before you return to the start?

8

● **5. a)** Draw the same sequence with right turns.

● **b)** Is it the same as the pattern you drew for **4** or not?

● **6.** What pattern do you think you would get if you used the sequence 4, 2, 8 right? Try it and see if you are right.

● **7.** What happens to this spirobot?

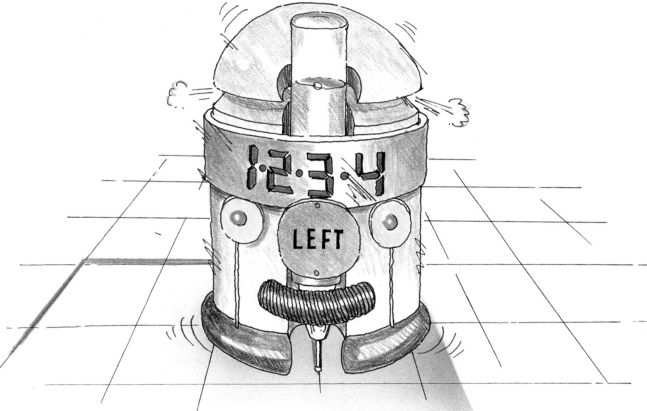

● **8.** Find another sequence where the same thing happens.

● Investigate using different number sequences. Try mixing left and right turns. Does the pattern for your date of birth return to the start?

If you have a computer with Turtle graphics or Logo, you can use it to draw the patterns. Multiply the numbers by ten so that the pattern is large enough to see. Remember that you will need to program in a turn after each move.

Answers to pages 8 and 9

3. The spirobot repeats the program four times.

4. a) Your pattern should look like this.

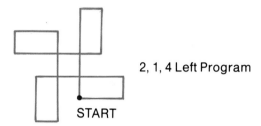

2, 1, 4 Left Program

START

4. b) The sequence repeats four times.

5. a) This is the sequence with right turns.

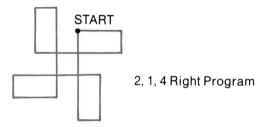

START

2, 1, 4 Right Program

5. b) It is a **reflection** of the previous pattern.

6. You get the same pattern as for 2, 1, 4 right, but each line is twice as long.

7. The spirobot will carry on to infinity or until it wears out.

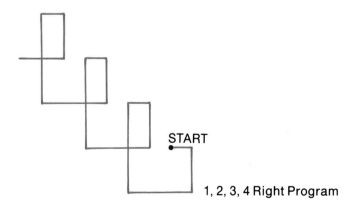

START

1, 2, 3, 4 Right Program

8. 1, 2, 3, 4 left is another possible sequence that never returns to the starting point.

Fun with Grids

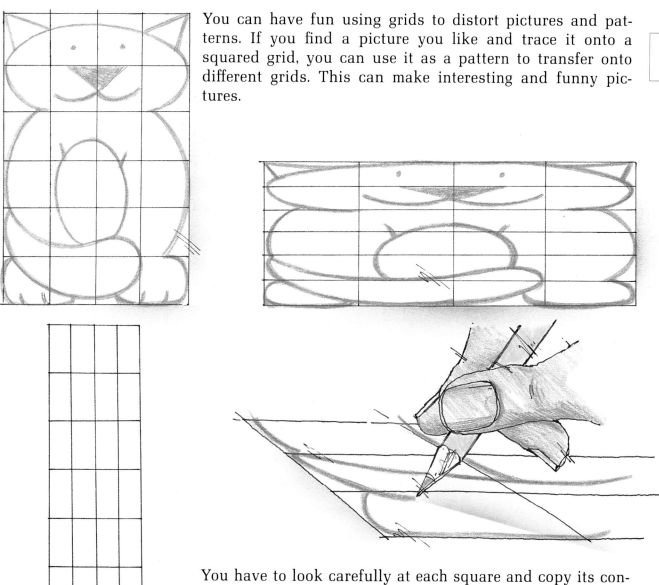

You can have fun using grids to distort pictures and patterns. If you find a picture you like and trace it onto a squared grid, you can use it as a pattern to transfer onto different grids. This can make interesting and funny pictures.

11

You have to look carefully at each square and copy its contents in the matching shape on the grid.

Copy the picture of the cat on to a grid like the one shown right. Make your grid 6″ tall and 2″ wide. Do not draw on the book.

You can use all kinds of grids. Here are a few ideas.

Your copy of the cat should look like this.

Copy the cat on to some more of the grids or design a picture or pattern and copy it on to a grid of your own. Do not draw on the book.

Follow That Pattern

Each of these patterns is made by repeating a shape along a strip of graph paper two squares wide. Sometimes the shape is flipped over to make the pattern. On graph paper, copy and continue each pattern. For each pattern, identify the basic shape from which it is made.

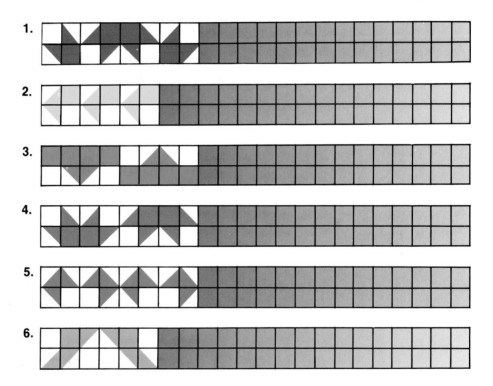

Using this shape, make as many different patterns as you can that will fit into a row two squares wide.

You can make up similar patterns to fill a square. These patterns use one basic shape, or motif, made from an area 3 squares wide and 3 squares high. The motif can be repeated to fit into a 6 by 6 square area. These are just some of the possibilities. Try some of your own.

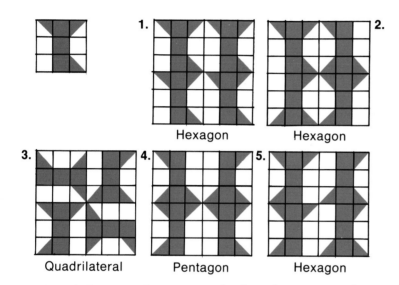

1. Hexagon

2. Hexagon

3. Quadrilateral

4. Pentagon

5. Hexagon

Notice the different shapes made by the gaps where the repeated motifs touch. In three of the designs, the gaps are **hexagons**. The other two are **quadrilaterals** and **pentagons**.

● Which is which?

◇ Each large 6 by 6 square can be repeated in many ways to make a larger pattern. Copy and complete this pattern to make a 12 by 12 square.

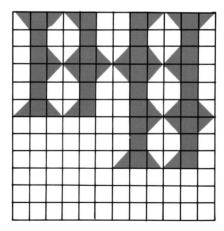

● Investigate making large patterns of your own, using one simple shape based on a 3 by 3 square.

Your pattern rows for page 13 should look like these.

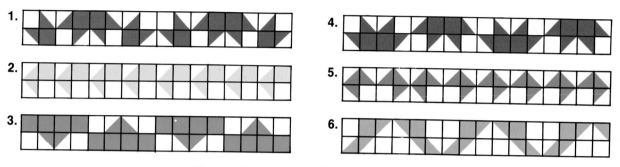

● If you did not get them right, try these.

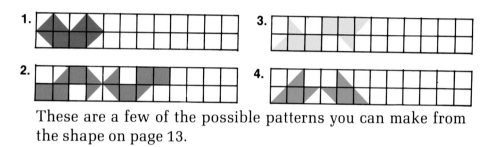

These are a few of the possible patterns you can make from the shape on page 13.

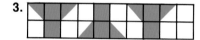

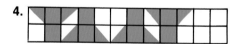

● Investigate making row patterns with shapes of your own. There is no need to stick to squares. If you use a copy of the triangular grid at the back of the book, it is easy to make patterns based on **equilateral** triangles or hexagons.

These simple patterns are based on an equilateral triangle.

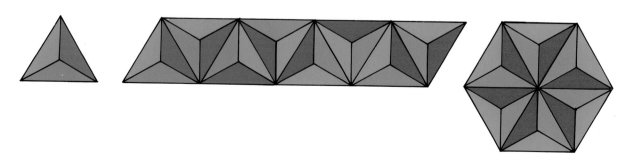

Seeing Stars

You need a copy of the grid of triangular dots at the back of the book.

Both of these patterns are based on this star shape.

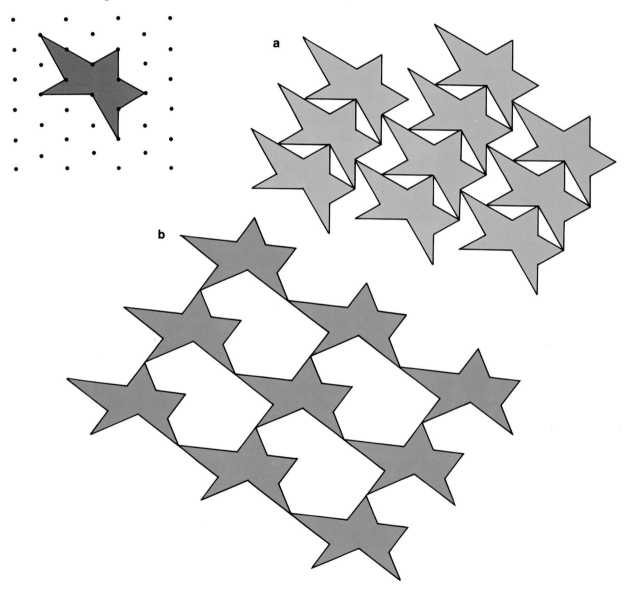

a

b

Copy the patterns on to a copy of the triangular grid and color them.

● **1.** Find a star in the middle of each pattern. At how many positions does it touch another star?

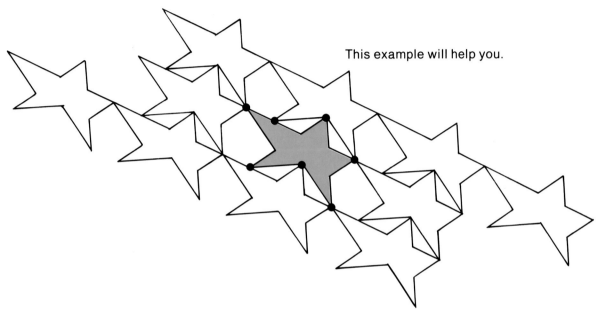

This example will help you.

● **2.** What are the names of the shapes made by the spaces between the stars?

● **3.** Investigate drawing your own patterns with the stars to make different shaped holes between them. Try other star shapes and see what happens. Experiment with stars on a square grid.

Squares and Holes

18 Cut out five 1″ squares from thin cardboard. Arrange them with corners touching to make a **pentagon** hole like this.

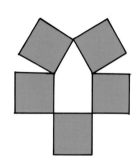

● **1.** Show how it is possible to arrange the five squares, **with corners touching**, to make **a)** a different pentagon, **b)** a **hexagon**, **c)** a **heptagon**, **d)** an **octagon** and **e)** a **pentangle**.

● **2.** What shapes are possible using only four squares?

◇ Investigate using more squares or a different shape such as a hexagon.

KEEP YOUR SQUARES: YOU WILL NEED THEM AGAIN.

Answers to page 14

In patterns 1, 2 and 5 the gaps between the motifs are hexagons. Pattern 3 makes quadrilaterals and pattern 4, pentagons.

This is the completed pattern of the 12 by 12 square.

Answers to page 17

1. In pattern **a)** there are eight positions where a star touches other stars. In pattern **b)** there are four.

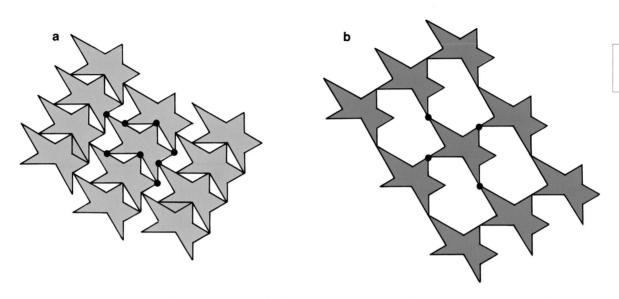

2. In pattern **a)** the holes are triangles and **pentagons**. In pattern **b)** they are **octogons**.

3. Here are three more possible patterns.

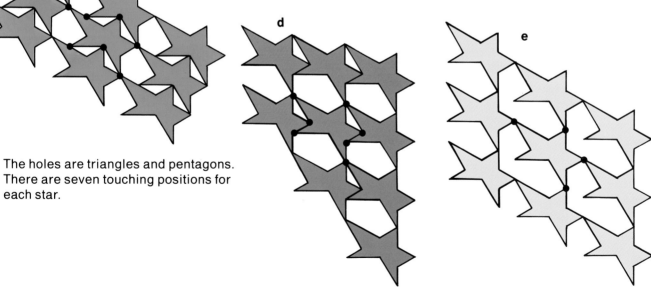

The holes are triangles and pentagons. There are seven touching positions for each star.

The holes are octogons. there are four touching positions for each star.

Answers to page 18

1. These are some of the possible answers.

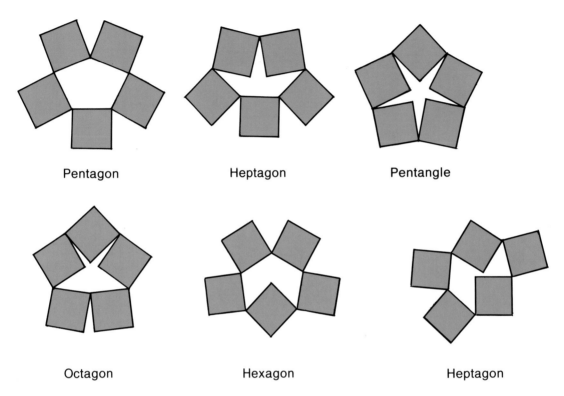

Pentagon   Heptagon   Pentangle

Octagon   Hexagon   Heptagon

◇ If you did not succeed in making the shapes, have another try at making a hexagon and a heptagon. Many different ones are possible.

2. You can make a square hole or a **rhombus** hole from four squares. The shape of the rhombus can change.

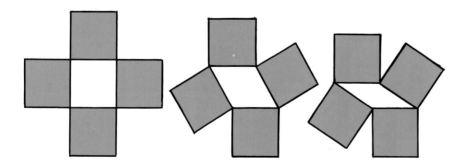

Pentominoes

Pentominoes are shapes made from five equal squares with *whole* sides touching.

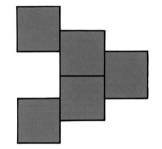

This is not a pentomino

This is not a pentomino

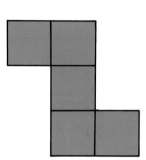

This is a pentomino

● Use your five cardboard squares from page 18 to make as many different pentominoes as you can. Record your answers on graph paper.

These all count as one pentomino. They are all the same shape turned around or flipped over.

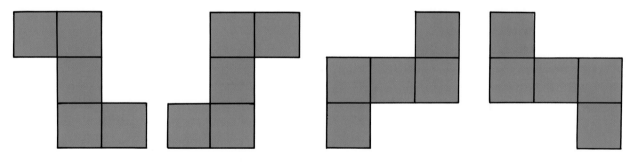

If you work according to a system you are more likely to find all the possibilities. For example, the pentomino above has a block of three squares with two more squares added on, one on each side. You can start by thinking about where else the two odd squares could go.

Is there any way of arranging the squares so you do not get a row of three?

There are five possible tetrominoes, shapes made by joining four squares edge to edge. Copy them with the same size squares as your pentominoes and cut them out.

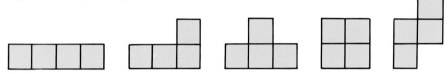

- Use one of your pentominoes with the five tetrominoes to make a 5 by 5 square.

Omino games for two

Game 1

- Make a set of cardboard pentominoes. Check the answers to page 21 to make sure you have a full set. Draw an 8 by 8 board of the same size squares as the pentominoes. Squares with $\frac{1}{2}$″ sides are a good size.

Take turns to pick a pentomino until they are all gone.

Toss a coin to see who starts. The other player starts the next game, and from then you take turns to start.

Take turns laying a pentomino on the board until it is impossible to lay down any more. If one player cannot lay down a piece, the other player can have another turn.

The pentominoes must not overlap. Pentominoes must cover whole squares. You may turn pentominoes around and flip them over. Once you have put a pentomino in position on the board, you must not move it.

The player with the fewest pentominoes left is the winner.

These pieces are left. Red and blue cannot lay, the game is drawn.

Game 2

Choose just one pentomino each and make six copies. Take turns laying them down using the same rules as in game 1. The player with the fewest pentominoes left is the winner.

Green wins.
There is only one green pentomino not on the boad.
Yellow has two pentominoes left but cannot lay them.

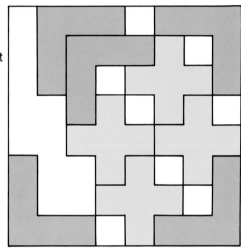

Game 3

Play with a full set of pentominoes. Take turns using the same rules as in game 1, but this time without a board. Score a point for each square of another pentomino that you touch with your pentomino.

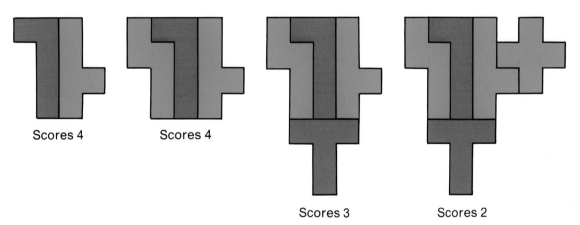

Scores 4   Scores 4   Scores 3   Scores 2

You must not overlap, but you can leave gaps. Only whole squares score. The winner is the one with the highest total score at the end of the game.

Game 4

Take turns choosing pentominoes. Each player has one minute to arrange all the pieces to fit as nearly as possible into a 5 by 6 rectangle. Pentominoes must not overlap, but they can be turned around and flipped over. Every square outside the rectangle counts as 1 point. The winner is the one with the **lowest** score.

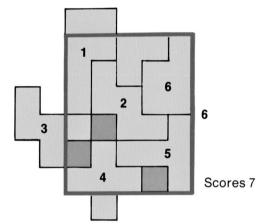

Scores 4

Scores 7

Answers to pages 21 and 22

There are twelve pentominoes.

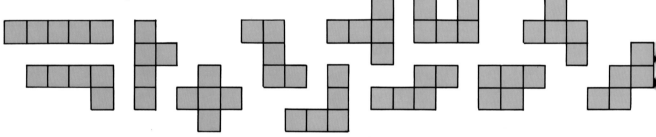

This is one way of forming a 5 by 5 square with one pentomino and all the tetrominoes. There are other possibilities, too.

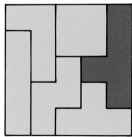

KEEP YOUR PENTOMINOES. YOU WILL NEED THEM AGAIN.

Ways of Making Patterns

You have been making patterns with shapes by moving them in different ways. You can move a shape three ways.

Translation

You can repeat a shape the same way around in a new position. This is called **translation**. It is a common way of repeating patterns on wallpapers and fabrics.

Rotation

You can turn a shape around. Often in patterns, shapes are turned 90° or 180°, but you can turn as much or as little as you wish.

This pattern, which the Romans used on their mosaic floors, is made by rotating a simple square pattern to form a pattern of four squares.

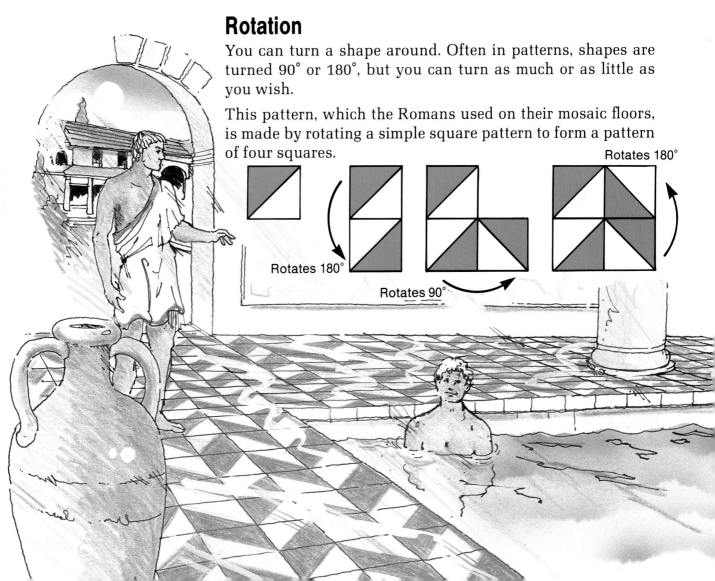

Reflection

You can flip a shape over so that it looks like what you would see if you reflected the shape in a mirror; you make a mirror image. Sometimes this is easy, but don't forget that you have to reverse all the details on a complicated figure.

26

● The artist has made four deliberate mistakes in the reflections. Can you spot them?

Some patterns use combinations of translation, reflection and rotation. In the Roman mosaic floor pattern on the previous page, each block of four squares is translated to enlarge the pattern.

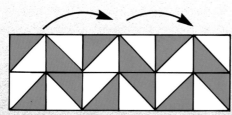

The block of four squares is translated.

Lines of Symmetry

28

Some shapes and objects look exactly the same if you put a mirror halfway across them.

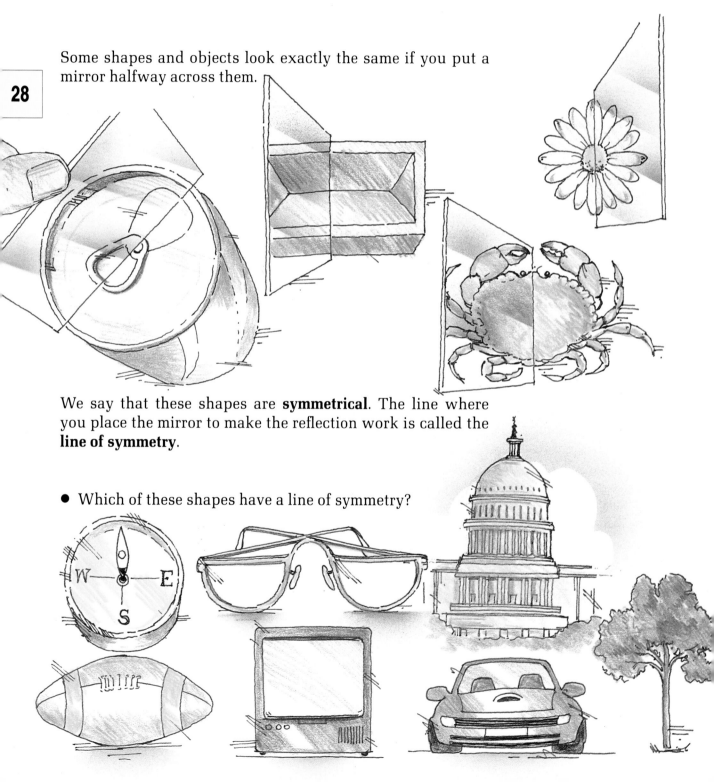

We say that these shapes are **symmetrical**. The line where you place the mirror to make the reflection work is called the **line of symmetry**.

● Which of these shapes have a line of symmetry?

Our bodies look symmetrical at first glance, but they are not exactly so.

Our faces are not exactly symmetrical either. Some are almost perfectly symmetrical. Usually we find these more pleasing than faces that are very lopsided.

● Can you identify these famous faces? There are two in each picture. Use your mirror if you need some help.

1. and 2.

3. and 4.

Answers to page 28

These are the shapes with a line of symmetry.
The line of symmetry has been drawn in for you.

Some shapes and objects have more than one line of symmetry. A snowflake has six lines of symmetry.

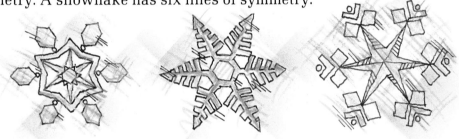

● How many lines of symmetry does each of these drawings have?

The natural objects such as the apple, the flower, the butterfly and the lemon have been drawn symmetrically. If you look carefully at the real things, however, you will see that just as we are not perfectly symmetrical, neither are other living things. If you cut an apple in half, the seeds will not be all quite the same size or exactly evenly spaced.

Mathematical shapes, however, can be perfectly symmetrical. Often an easy way to find the lines of symmetry in a shape is to fold it.

If you can fold a shape so that one half fits exactly on top of the other, then you have found a line of symmetry.

Cut a square from graph paper.

● **1.** How many fold lines can you find so that one half fits exactly on top of the other?

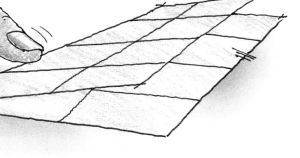

● **2.** How many lines of symmetry does the square have?

● **3.** Is the number of lines of symmetry the same for all squares?

Cut out a copy of this **parallelogram**.

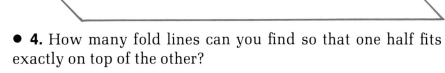

● **4.** How many fold lines can you find so that one half fits exactly on top of the other?

● **5.** How many lines of symmetry does the parallelogram have?

● **6.** Is it the same for all parallelograms?

● **7.** How many lines of symmetry does an **equilateral** triangle have?

Use a copy of this equilateral triangle to help you.

Answers to page 30

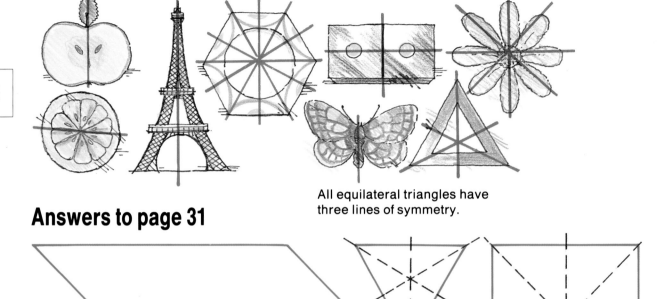

All equilateral triangles have three lines of symmetry.

Answers to page 31

The parallelogram has no lines of symmetry. It is the same for all parallelograms.

The square has four lines of symmetry. The number is the same for all squares.

If you did not get these right, make the folds and check that they really work before you try the rest of the shapes on this page.

● Copy these shapes, do not draw lines on the book. How many lines of symmetry do these shapes have?

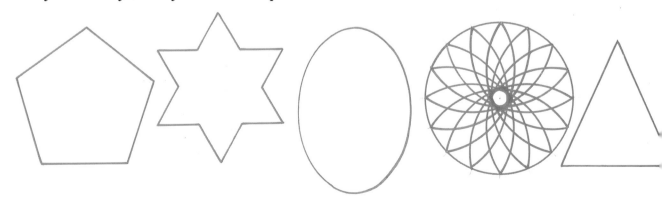

Pentominoes and line symmetry

Look again at your set of pentominoes.

● **1.** How many lines of symmetry does each one have?

● **2.** Pick out the ones that have no line of symmetry. There are six. Arrange them to form two shapes that have at least one line of symmetry.

3. If you reflect a pentomino in a mirror placed on one of its edges you get a new shape.

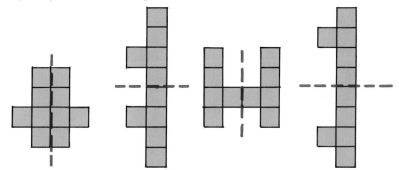

● Draw all the possible new shapes made by reflecting one of your pentominoes, using vertical and horizontal lines of symmetry on the edges of the pentomino.

● **4.** Look at the other pentominoes. How many different shapes is it possible to make for each of them if you use the same rule about only vertical and horizontal lines of symmetry on their edges. Reflections and rotations do not count as different shapes for this investigation.

KEEP YOUR RESULTS, YOU WILL NEED THEM AGAIN.

● **5.** How many lines of symmetry do these patterns have?

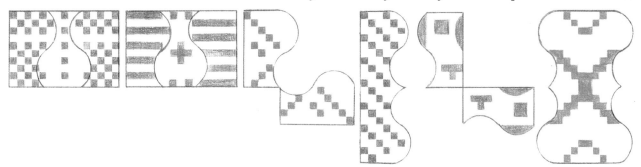

◇ Experiment with making your own patterns on graph paper.

Answers to page 32

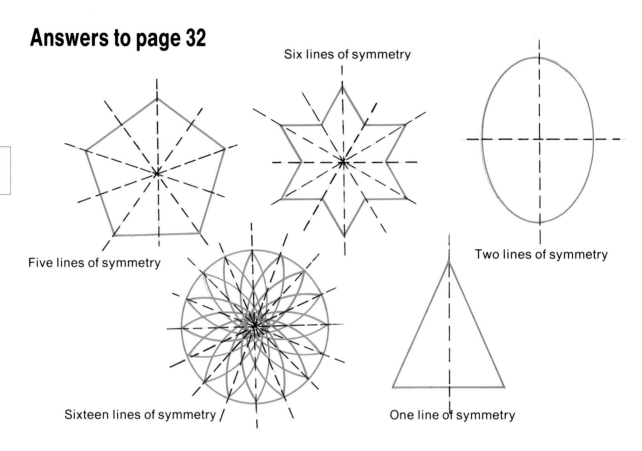

Six lines of symmetry

Five lines of symmetry

Two lines of symmetry

Sixteen lines of symmetry

One line of symmetry

Answers to page 33

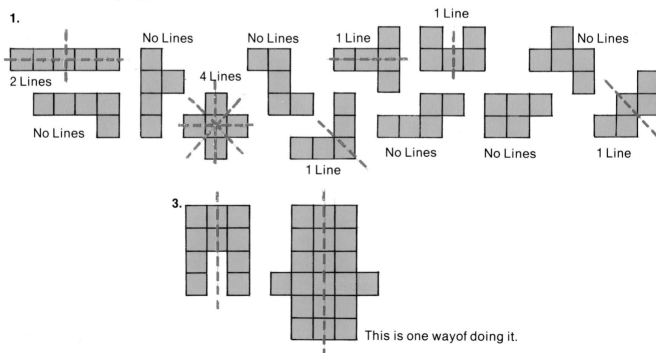

1.

2 Lines

No Lines

No Lines

4 Lines

No Lines

1 Line

1 Line

No Lines

1 Line

No Lines

No Lines

1 Line

3.

This is one way of doing it.

4.

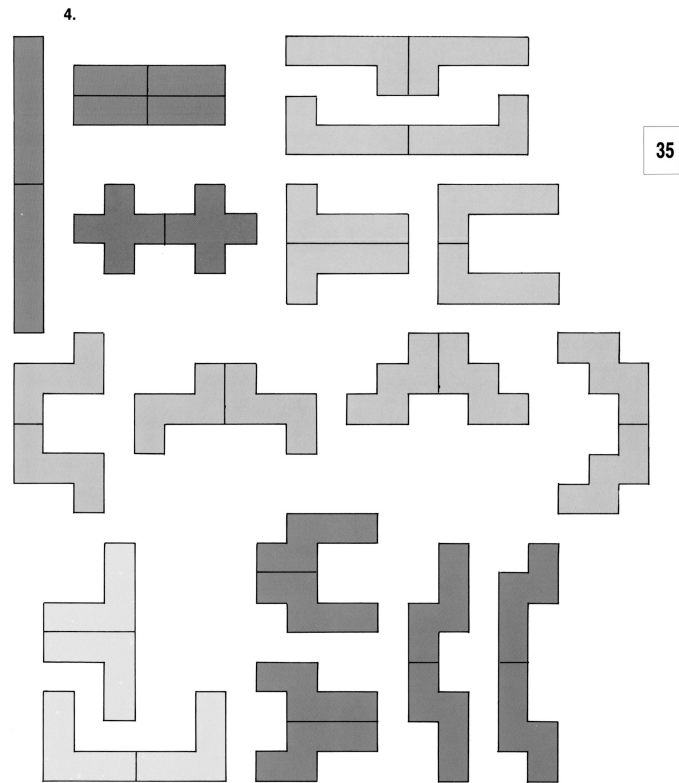

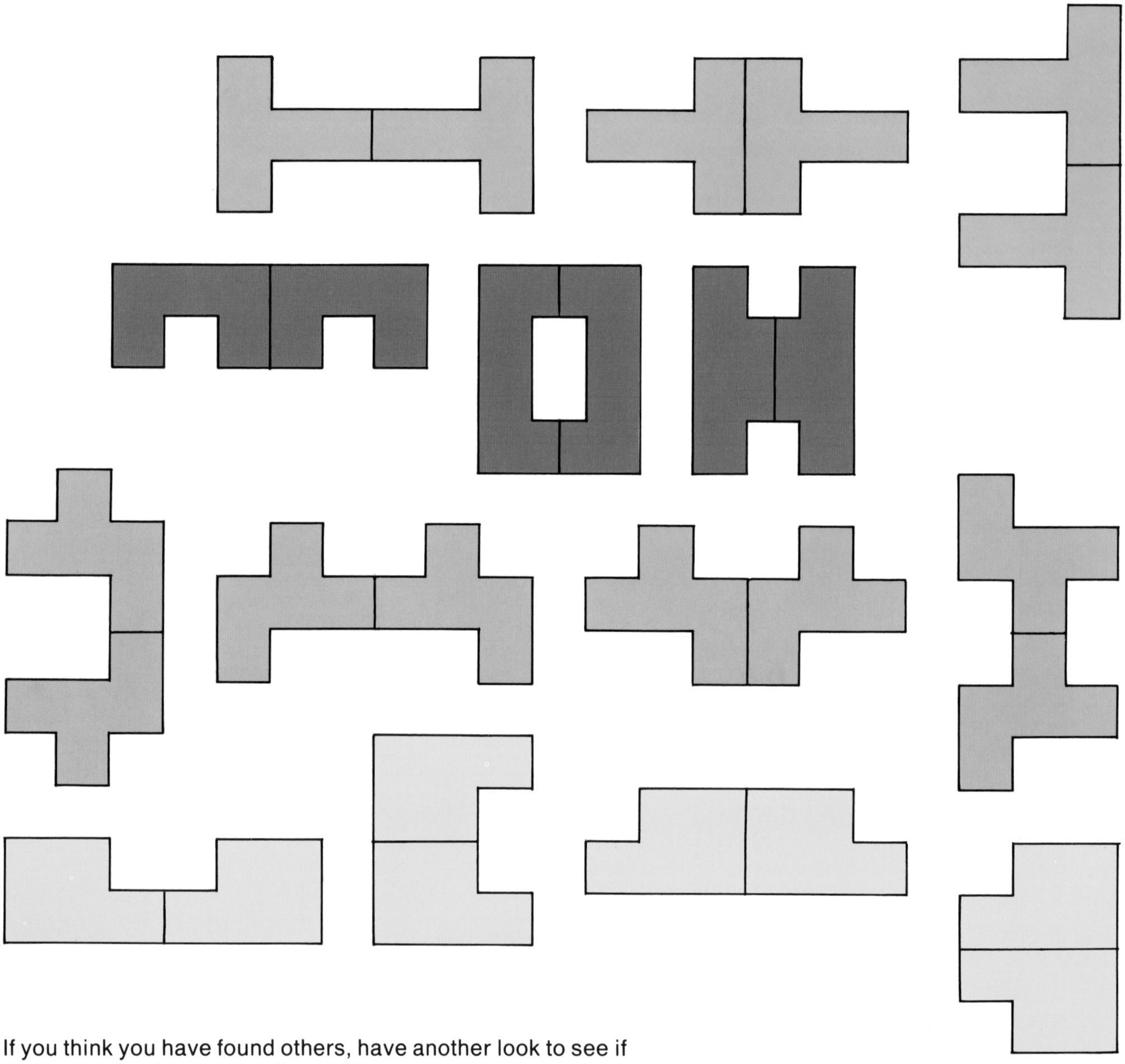

36

If you think you have found others, have another look to see if
they are reflections or rotations of these.

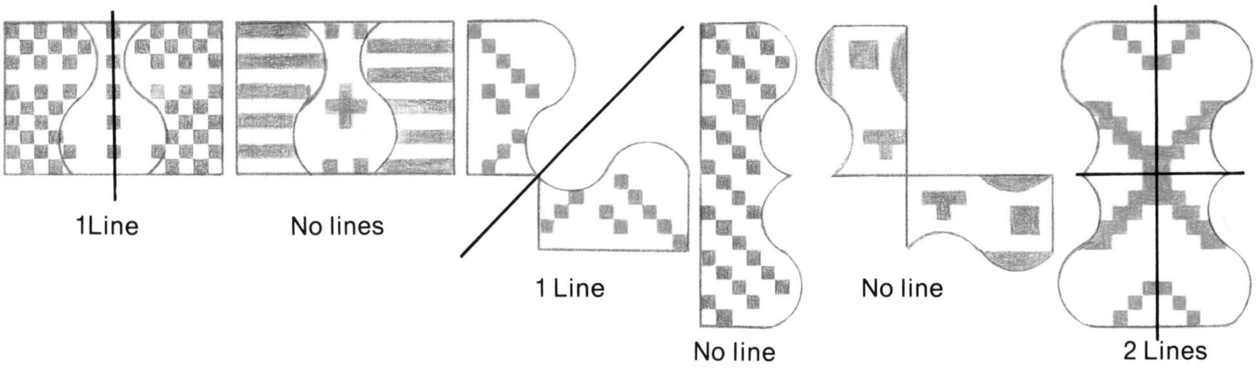

1Line

No lines

1 Line

No line

No line

2 Lines

Rotational Symmetry

The windmill and letter S look symmetrical, but they do not have lines of symmetry.

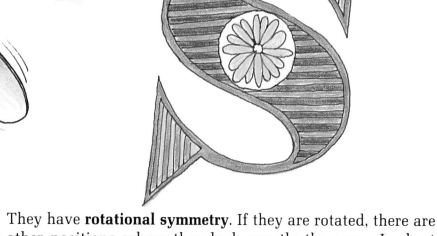

They have **rotational symmetry**. If they are rotated, there are other positions where they look exactly the same. Look at this lid – it can fit on the container three different ways and yet it looks the same each time. It has rotational symmetry of order 3.

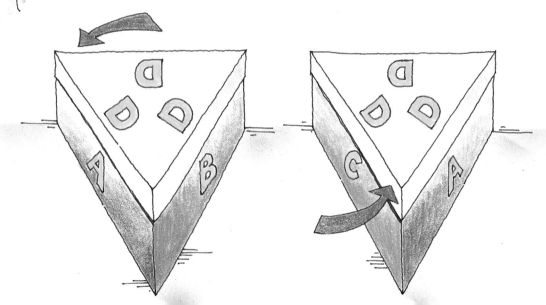

The minimum order of rotational symmetry for a symmetrical figure is 2. If a figure has an order of rotational symmetry of 1 then it is not symmetrical.

If you have a drawing on a page, it is not always easy to see how many ways you can turn it so that it still looks the same.

To find the rotational order of symmetry of the designs on the plates below, trace the design. Hold the tracing paper in the center of the plate and rotate it all the way round the plate. The number of times the pattern on the tracing fits over the pattern on the plate is the order of rotational symmetry.

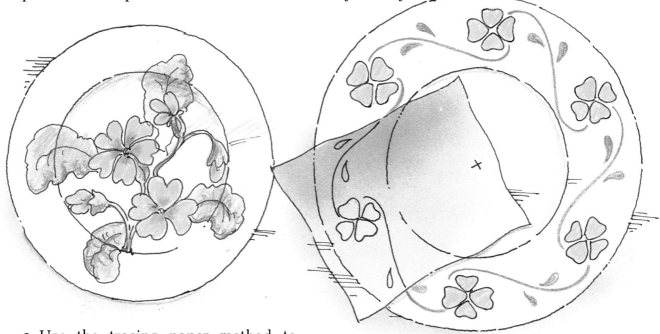

● Use the tracing paper method to find what order of rotational symmetry each of the objects on the previous page has. You will see that the two objects with two lines of symmetry or more have rotational symmetry as well.

● Can you explain why this shape, which has no lines of symmetry, only made two possible reflections on page 34, while all the other pentominoes with no lines of symmetry made four different reflections?

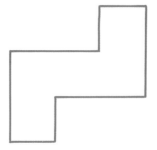

Symmetry and Color

When you are looking for symmetry, color is as important as shape. This uncolored hexagon pattern has six lines of symmetry and rotational symmetry of order 6.

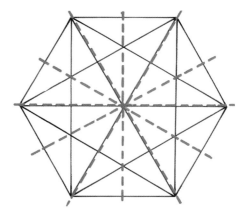

You can see how changing the way it is colored changes the number of lines of symmetry and the order of rotational symmetry.

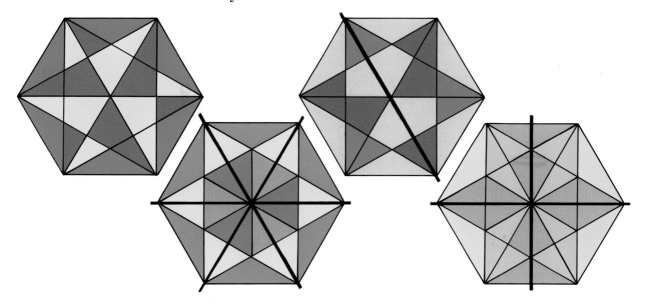

● How many lines and what order of symmetry does each of these patterns have?

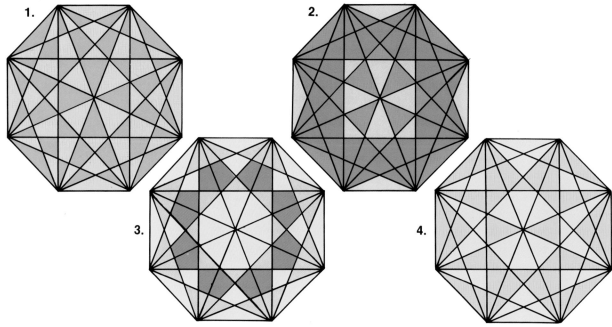

1. **2.** **3.** **4.**

◇ Investigate lines and orders of symmetry by drawing and coloring patterns of your own.

The circle is an interesting shape to think about in relation to line and rotational symmetry. A plain circle with no pattern or color has more lines and more orders of symmetry than any other shape. Any line that passes through the center from one point to another on the **circumference** is a line of symmetry.

You can draw an infinite number of lines through the center, so the circle has an infinite number of lines of symmetry. The circle can also be rotated an infinite number of ways and still look the same.

◇ Try drawing a sequence of circles from ones with no lines of symmetry, one line, two lines and so on, to as many as you can. You will eventually have lines so close together that you will have to give up. If you could draw infinitely fine lines, you could go on forever!

◇ When you increase the number of lines of symmetry, what effect does it have on the order of rotational symmetry.

Answers to page 33

These are the six pentominoes that have no line of symmetry.

2.

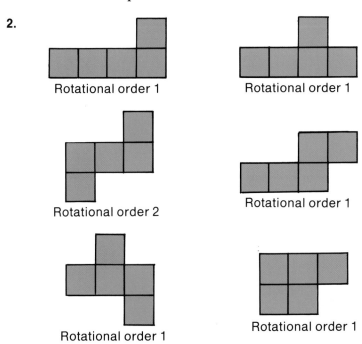

Rotational order 1   Rotational order 1

Rotational order 2   Rotational order 1

Rotational order 1   Rotational order 1

Answers to page 38

The windmill and the letter S both have rotational symmetry order 2.

The reason the pentomino had fewer reflections was that it had rotational symmetry of order 2. The others with no lines of symmetry had no rotational symmetry either, so every possible reflection made a different shape.

Mirror Codes

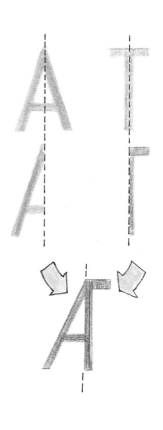

● **1.** Each of these shapes has been made by cutting two symmetrical letters of the alphabet in half and putting the two halves together. One example has been done to show you how it works. See if you can draw the two complete letters in each case.

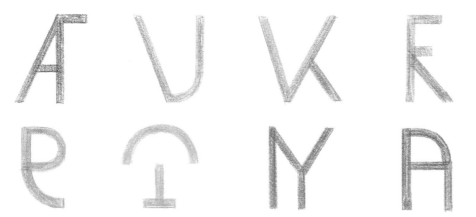

You can write in mirror code by only writing half of each symmetrical letter. A becomes **/** and B is written **ᗞ**.

● **2.** What do these say in mirror code?

ᕫ I ᙠ   ᒣ ᑌ ᒪ   ᗞ ᙁ ᐯ

ᐯ ᖴ ᐱ ᒪ   ᐯ ᖴ ᐱ   ᒣ ᒪ ᙁ

ᙁ ᙁ   ᙏ ᙁ ᒪ   ᒣ ᖴ ᐯ ᒪ   I ᒪ ᗩ

● **3.** Write out the symmetrical letters of the alphabet and make up some messages of your own. You can do the same thing with numbers and sums. Are these correct or not?

ᗝ ᗝ ᆂ II ᒪ ᗝ   I ᗝ ᒪ I ᓀ I   ᗝ ᆂ I I ᒪ ᗝ   ᓀ ᒪ ᐯ ᒪ ᓀ ᒪ ᗝ ᗝ

Completing Reflections

It is usually pretty easy to complete a symmetrical shape when you are given half of it and a line of symmetry. You can draw it free-hand. Or, if it is on a piece of paper, you can fold the paper on the symmetry line and prick through important points of the design with a pin. A third method is to make a tracing and then flip the tracing over on the line.

43

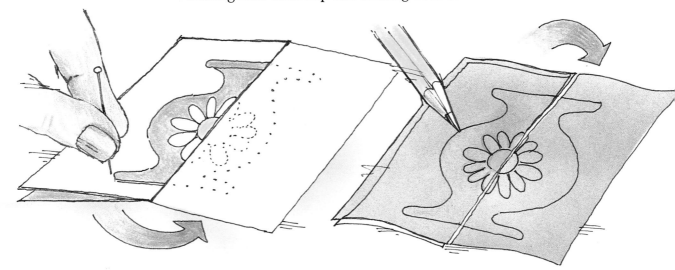

◇ Use tracing paper to copy and complete these.

Reflections Without Drawing

44

You can make reflections without drawing at all.

Paint patterns

This can be messy, so wear an apron and use plenty of newspaper to protect the area where you are working. Load a brush with paint and shake it over a clean piece of paper. Fold the paper and press down firmly. Open up the paper again to see what symmetrical pattern you have created. You can experiment to find the best consistency of paint. You can try mixing colors and changing where you make the fold lines.

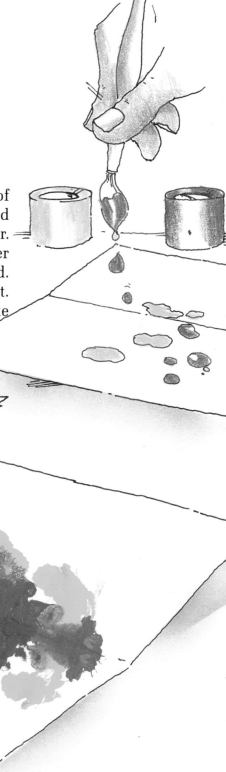

Scissors patterns

Fold a piece of paper diagonally in half. If the paper is not square, cut off the extra paper to make it square. Take care to make the edges meet exactly.

You now have a triangle. Fold it in half. Fold the new triangle in half again. Carefully cut out shapes along the fold lines. Be careful to keep the folded edges together. When you have finished cutting, gently unfold the paper to discover the pattern.

◇ How many lines of symmetry does your pattern have? What is the order of symmetry?

◇ Experiment with different shapes and different folds. If you draw around a plate and make many careful folds, you can make some very intricate designs. You can make them in colored paper and use them as doilies, or make them in white paper and mount them on colored paper to decorate your room.

Finding Lines of Symmetry

You can ususally draw in lines of symmetry easily. Use tracing paper to find the lines of symmetry between these pairs. Trace the pair of objects and then fold the tracing so that one object exactly fits the other.

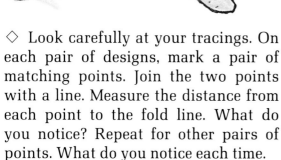

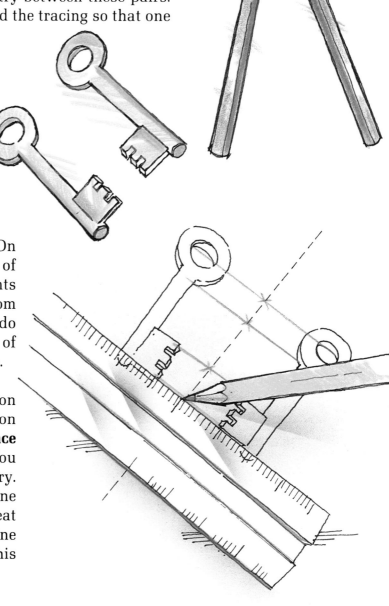

◇ Look carefully at your tracings. On each pair of designs, mark a pair of matching points. Join the two points with a line. Measure the distance from each point to the fold line. What do you notice? Repeat for other pairs of points. What do you notice each time.

You have found that for every point on a shape there is a matching point on its mirror image **at the same distance away from the line of symmetry**. You can always find a line of symmetry. Join two matching points with a line and mark the halfway point. Repeat for another pair of points. Draw a line through the two halfway points. This is the line of symmetry.

Bits and Pieces

When the early European settlers first tried to make their homes in America, they were very short of materials and cash and had to make the most of what they had. The settlers made the most of fabrics by recycling them. They cut up worn out items and saved the best pieces to use again. These were carefully cut into pieces of the same shape and size. Women then sewed the pieces together to form patchwork quilts.

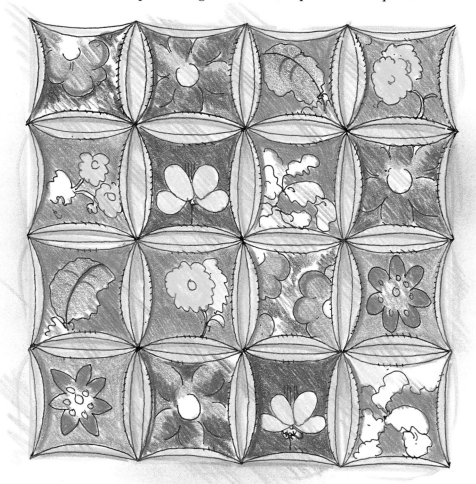

It is said that this design originated when the women of the *Mayflower* used flour sacks as backing for precious, tiny scraps of fabric.

What began as an economy measure has developed over the years to an art and a source of pleasure for many people. You can find beautiful quilts with traditional and modern designs in American homes and museums.

In fact, making patchwork goes back much further than the eighteenth century. Patchwork clothes were worn as early as the twelfth century in Europe. At the same time, and particularly in the fourteenth and fifteenth centuries, stone masons and artists used the same method of cutting simple shapes to create beautifully patterned floors in Italian churches.

48

Both patchwork and tiled floors often use one or two simple shapes which are repeated to completely fill or cover an area. There are no spaces between the shapes and the pattern can be endlessly continued. In mathematics this kind of pattern is called a **tessellation**.

Tiling with Quadrilaterals

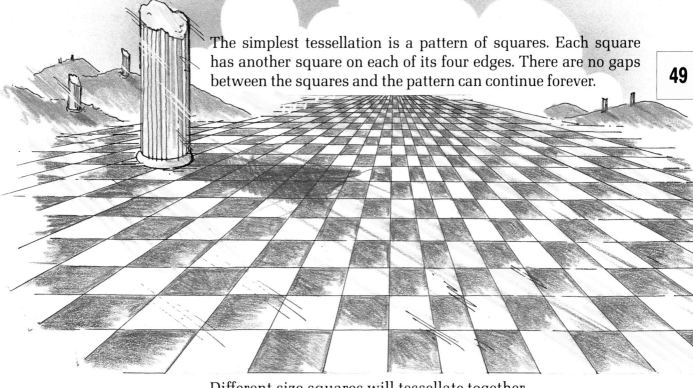

The simplest tessellation is a pattern of squares. Each square has another square on each of its four edges. There are no gaps between the squares and the pattern can continue forever.

49

Different size squares will tessellate together.

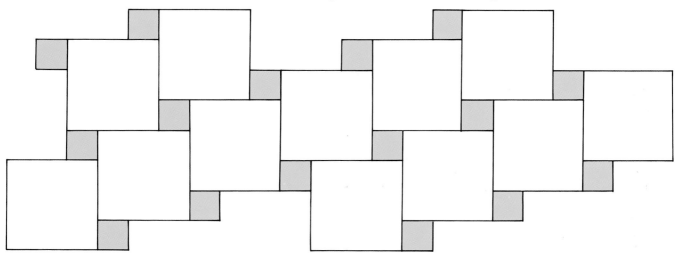

◇ Make a tessellation of your own with two different size squares.

50

● Mark a cross on the top right-hand corner of each small square in your tessellation. Join up the crosses. What do you notice?

The square is a **regular quadrilateral**. Any convex quadrilateral will make a tiling pattern. (A convex quadrilateral has no angles greater than 180°.) This tiling pattern is made from an irregular quadrilateral.

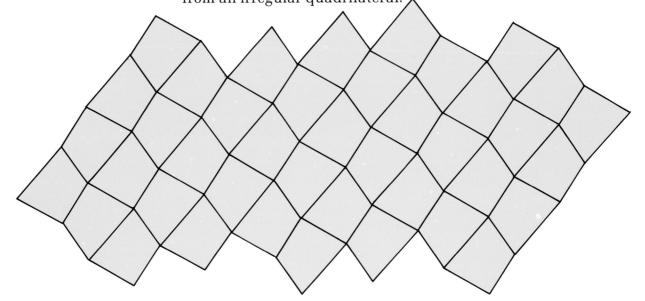

When you color it this way, you can see more clearly what shape the tile is.

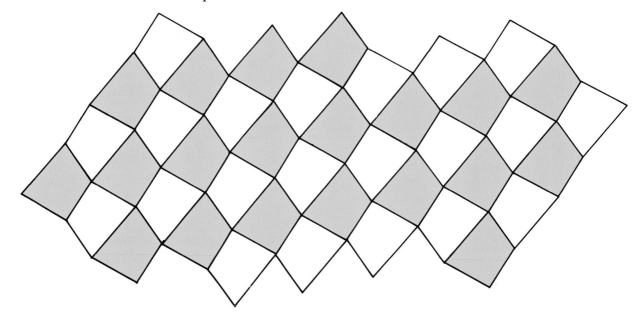

You can emphasize different ways of looking at the pattern by the way you color it.

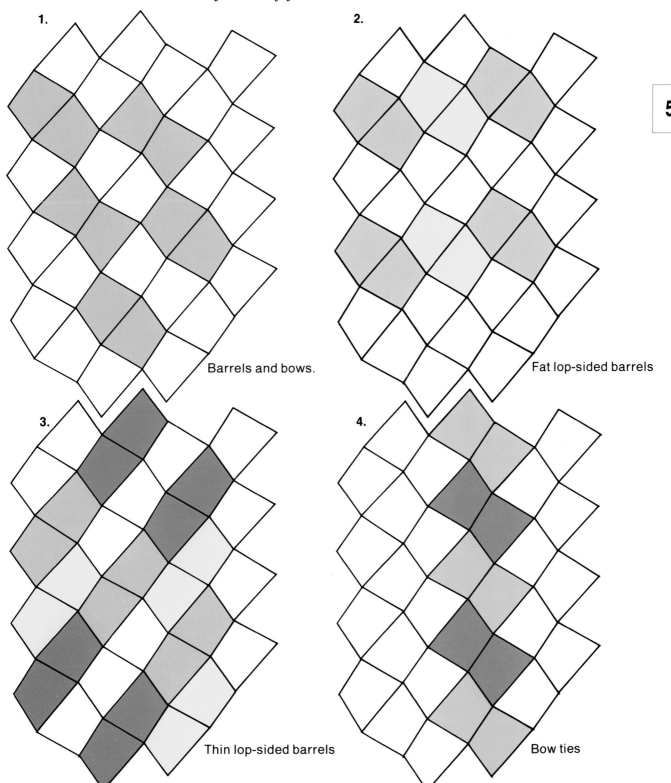

1.

Barrels and bows.

2.

Fat lop-sided barrels

3.

Thin lop-sided barrels

4.

Bow ties

You have to turn the tile 180° degrees each time to make an irregular quadrilateral tessellate. The same angle is colored blue in this block of four tiles. You can see how it rotates 180° from one tile to the next.

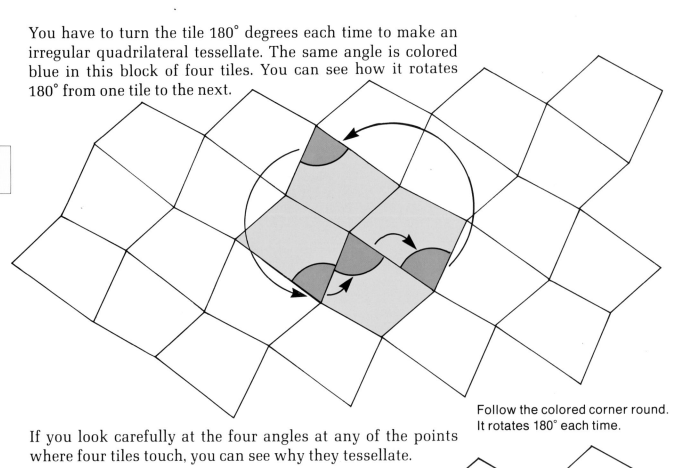

Follow the colored corner round. It rotates 180° each time.

If you look carefully at the four angles at any of the points where four tiles touch, you can see why they tessellate.

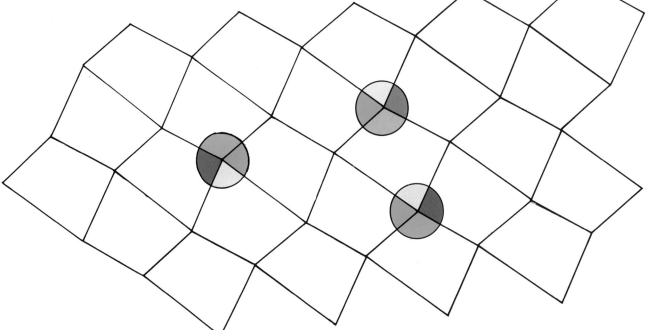

At any point where four tiles meet, there is one each of the four angles of the pattern tile. The sum of the angles round a point is 360° The sum of the angles of a quadrilaterals is 360°

This pattern creates a three-dimensional effect of looking through a grille. It uses a square and a trapezoid.

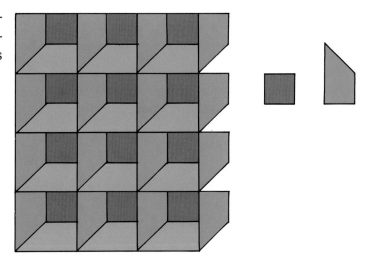

These two patterns use the same tile – a **rhombus**.

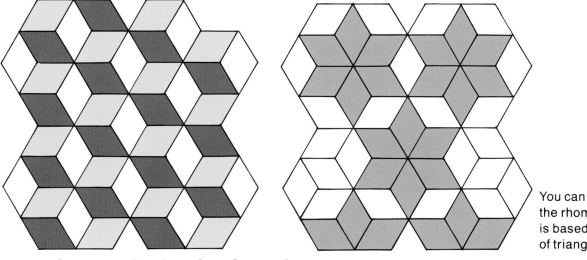

You can see that the rhombus tile is based on a grid of triangles.

● Use the triangular dotted grid to make your own version and color it however you like.

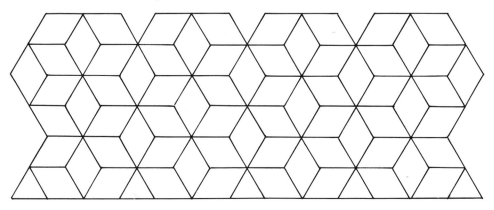

Two different rhombuses will tessellate.

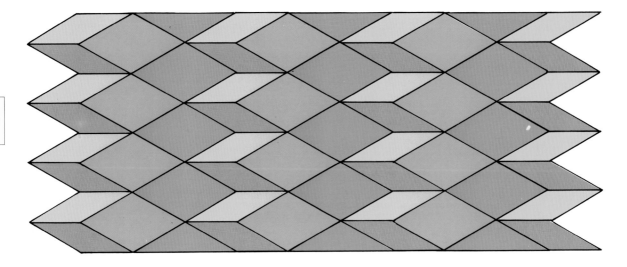

54

You can cut pieces off one side of a tile and add them on to the opposite side to make interesting tiling patterns.

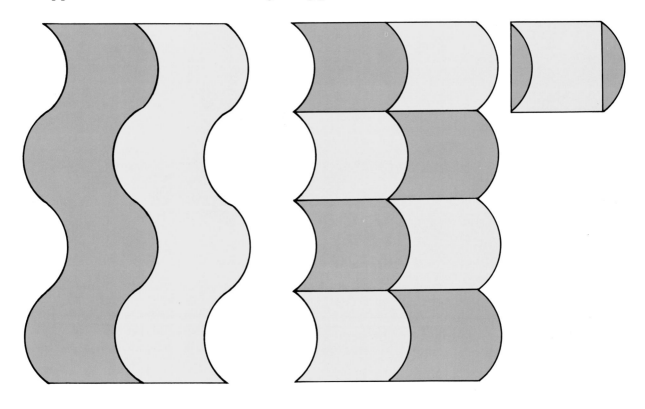

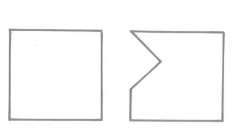

Try experimenting with
your own animal tiles.

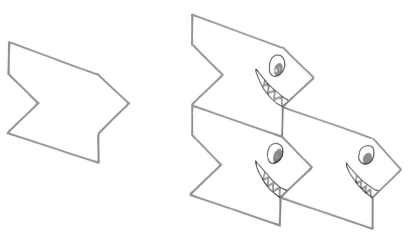

Tessellating with Other Shapes

● Copy the triangular and square dotted paper on pages 58
and 59. Use them to help you to find shapes other than
quadrilaterals or variations on quadrilaterals that will make
tiling patterns.

Triangles
The grid is made of equilateral triangles, so obviously they
tessellate.

● **1.** Do different size equilateral triangles tessellate in the
same way as different size squares?

● **2.** Do **scalene** triangles tessellate?

Pentagons
● **3.** Do **regular** pentagons tessellate?

● **4.** Do other pentagons tessellate?

Hexagons
● **5.** Do regular hexagons tessellate?

● **6.** Do other hexagons tessellate?

Octagons

- **7.** Do regular octagons tessellate?

- **8.** Do any octagons tessellate?

◇ **9.** You can continue investigating different polygons. See if you can find any connections between the irregular polygons that tessellate and quadrilaterals and triangles.

The ancient Romans were experts at making patterned floors. They made hundreds of patterns which looked different from each other but were in fact all based on a grid of squares. Each square in the framework was filled with small pieces of different colored stone. These stones were called "tesserae" and our word "tessellation" for special kinds of tiling patterns come from this.

The patterns in Celtic illuminated manuscripts and on Celtic stone crosses look very different from American bedspreads or Roman floors, but they too are based on repeating patterns in a square grid.

Hindu Rangoli patterns take a pattern in a square and reflect it.

The small square is reflected to form a larger square, which is in turn, reflected.

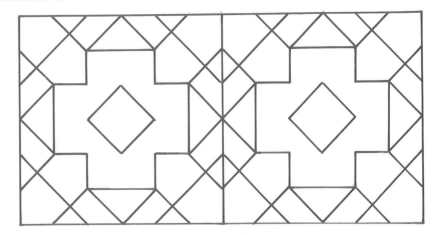

Islamic designs use circles and squares in a repeating pattern.

● **10.** Are there any other pairs of regular polygons, besides squares and triangles, that tessellate together?

11. Investigate tessellating curved shapes by altering the sides of a square or triangular grid.

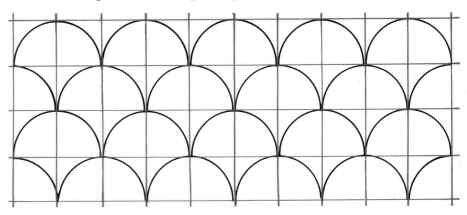

● Both these tiling patterns are based on hexagons on a triangular grid. Can you see how to make them?

1.

2.

Answers to page 55

1. Yes, different size equilateral triangles will tessellate. Here are two ways of doing it. There are other ways.

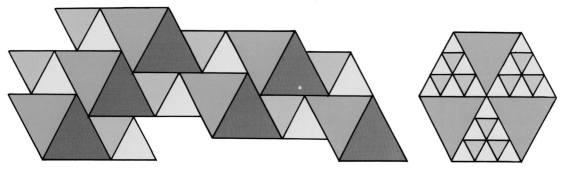

2. Yes, scalene triangles will tessellate. Here is one example.

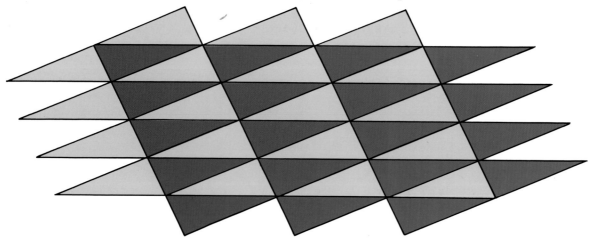

Square grid

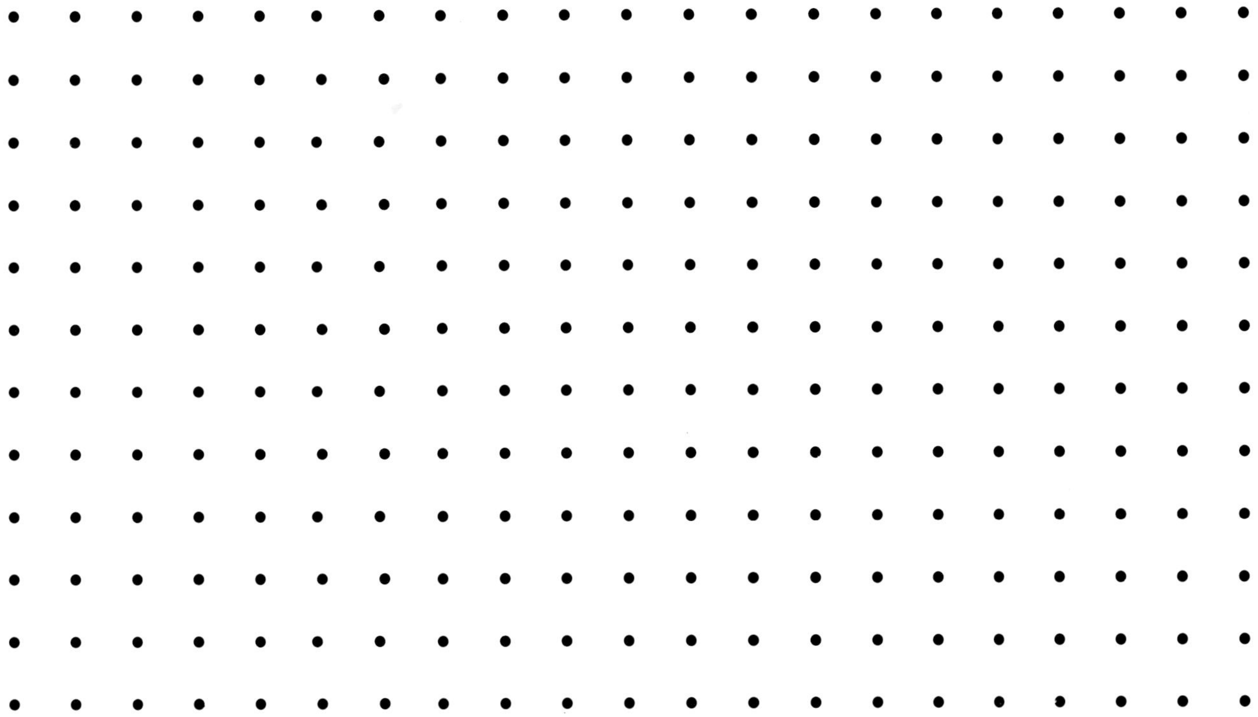

Triangular grid

Glossary

circumference   the distance around the edge of a circle

closed   a closed shape has no gaps in its sides

equilateral   an equilateral triangle has three equal sides and three equal angles of 60″

heptagon   a seven-sided polygon

hexagon   a six-sided polygon

line of symmetry   a line that divides a shape into two halves which are mirror images of each other

octagon   an eight-sided polygon

order of symmetry   the number of times a shape or pattern can be turned and still fill the same "hole," the number of different positions in which a tracing will fit exactly over it

parallelogram   a four-sided polygon with two pairs of equal and parallel sides

pentagon   a five-sided polygon

pentangle   a five-pointed star

polygon   a closed shape with straight sides

quadrilateral   a four-sided polygon

reflection   the mirror image of a shape or pattern

regular   a regular shape is one in which all the angles are equal and all the sides are equal

rhombus   a four-sided polygon with two pairs of parallel sides all of equal length. A square is a rhombus with right angles.

right angle   an angle of 90°, a quarter turn

rotation   the image formed by turning a shape or pattern a certain number of degrees

rotational symmetry   if a shape can be turned and still fill the same space, it has rotational symmetry

scalene   a scalene triangle has no equal angles or sides

symmetrical   a symmetrical shape or pattern has at least one line of symmetry, or rotational symmetry of order two or more

tessellation   a tiling pattern with no gaps between the tiles and that could be continued to infinity

translation   the image formed by moving a shape to another position

trapezoid   a quadrilateral with one pair of parallel sides

Answers

1.

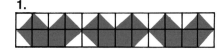

2.

3.

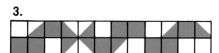

4.

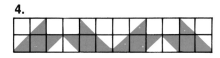

Page 26
No reflection of car.
No reflection of boat oar.
Reflection of clock tells wrong time.
Small spire reflection not colored.
Page 29
1. and **2.** Madonna and Princess Diana.
3. and **4.** Oliver Hardy and Stan Laurel.
Page 40

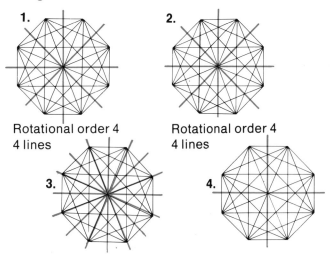

Rotational order 4
4 lines

Rotational order 4
4 lines

Rotational order 8
8 lines

Rotational order 2
2 lines

61

Page 41

These are some possible drawings.

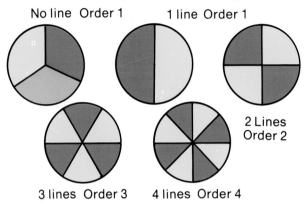

No line Order 1   1 line Order 1

2 Lines Order 2

3 lines Order 3   4 lines Order 4

Page 42

1 a. AT **b.** VU **c.** WX **d.** EK **e.** BC **f.** IO
g. NY **h.** HD
2 a. HID THE BOX
b. WHAT WAY TOM
c. DO YOU TAKE ICE
3 a. $88 \div 11 = 8$
b. $13 - 10 = 3$
c. $13 \times 0 = 0$
Each sum is correct.

Page 45

The pattern has four lines of symmetry and rotational symmetry of order 4.

Page 46

Each one of a pair of points is the same distance away from the fold line.

Page 50

A new grid of squares is formed.

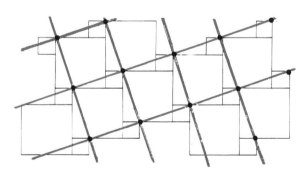

Page 55

1. See Page 58
2. See page 58.
3. A regular pentagon will not tessellate.
4. Here are two ways of tessellating one irregular pentagon.

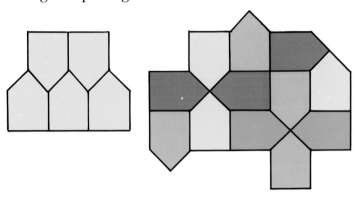

5. Regular hexagons tessellate.

6. These are tessellations of irregular hexagons. The quadrilateral tessellation on page 51 can also be looked at as a tessellation of two irregular hexagons.

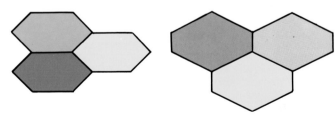

Page 56

7. Regular octagons will not tessellate on their own.

8. This is a tessellation of an irregular octagon.

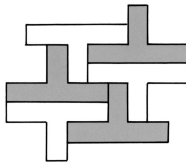

9. All the tessellations of irregular polygons can be broken down into quadrilaterals or triangles or a combination of the two.

Page 57

10. A regular octagon will tessellate with a square.

A regular decagon will tessellate with a square and a hexagon or with a triangle.

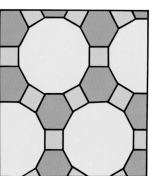
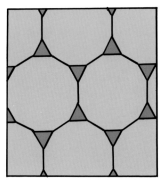

You can find many more fascinating tessellations.

Page 58

1.

These are the two tiles of tesselation.

Start by positioning hexagons like this with one dot between.

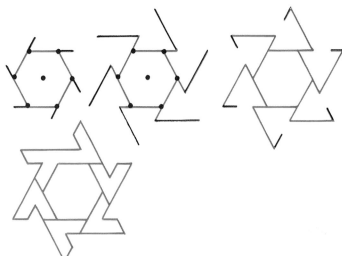

2.

a. Join six equilateral triangles to make a hexagon. Make each side of the triangle three dots long.

b. In each triangle, cut off one small triangle and add one on.

For this pattern the hexagons need to tessellate with each other.

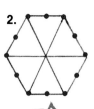

Index